Vale

Vale

Poems by

C. Walker

© 2024 C. Walker. All rights reserved.
This material may not be reproduced in any form, published,
reprinted, recorded, performed, broadcast,
rewritten, or redistributed without
the explicit permission of C. Walker.
All such actions are strictly prohibited by law.

Cover design by Shay Culligan
Cover image by Fabrizio Conti
Author image by Chris Wang

ISBN: 978-1-63980-587-7

Kelsay Books
502 South 1040 East, A-119
American Fork, Utah 84003
Kelsaybooks.com

To my cat and forever best friend, Bella.
To one of my biggest supporters, Selena.
To the boy I used to be.
To the man I am becoming.

Acknowledgments

The following poems have appeared first elsewhere, in the following journals or magazines:

The Raven Review: "A Drunkard's Ballad"
The Round: "Antigravity"
Third Wednesday: "This Is What You Want to Hear"

Foreword

This is an artistic collection about growth, about moving past the old, bringing in the new, and accepting change. This is a personal collection, but one that I believe many can relate to in some way. This is about a low point in my life and saying goodbye to it. The five sections walk you through the segments of change that I experienced. The first section is my overindulgence, the second is my cat Bella passing away unexpectedly, the third is a small break to address the big picture, the fourth section addresses my utter emotional collapse, and the fifth is the rebirth. I would hope that my suffering can become something beautiful through these pages you now hold. I would hope that those who have found themselves derailed can relate to these works and find solace. I would hope that the feelings of loss can eventually fade and the holes left in one's life be filled again. But the memories remain. And here they will slumber in ink.

Best wishes to you, reader.

C. Walker

Contents

I—Debauchery

Antigravity	15
A Drunkard's Ballad	16
Starry Hooched Man	17
Empty Cup of Cider	18

II—Desolation

Criticality	21
Split	22
I do not exist	23
Familial Craving	25

III—Diplomacy

the night that never ends	29
Hymn of the People	32
This Is What You Want to Hear	33
Untouched	34

IV—Destruction

Past the Beachgrass	37
Belong	38
To Answer the Call	39
That Glor'ous Sea	40

V—Development

Break Anew	49
Piano	50
On the Noon of My 20th Birthday	51
Bewildered	52

I—Debauchery

Antigravity

In the cup—there you go, take a sip
Now you're in the cup, but this cup
Loves disco—groove, baby, groove!
Foot shufflin, ear mufflin, drink sippin,
Take it all in, so close your eyes, then
Open to a world of antigravity
Space is what you make of it, and
I'm makin a cocktail called midnight
Just wait until the clock hammers
Pierced eyes with freed bliss, rhythm
Loose on the people, losing person
Gaining people, the whole world
Is in the palm of your eardrums
Thumpin, jammin melodies spill
Into your blood as you shake, shake,
Shake away from what was: thoughts
Pouring about you is the stench of
Now, you are at full bloom here,
Full moon, in the sky, ride it high
All night long; all night!

A Drunkard's Ballad

Sullen is the unmouthed word, the lonely love,
Tragedy the ne'er writ book, the ne'er sung song;
Hopeless is the flight that fell from high above,
Agony the sick and weak that were once strong.

This we say when life has gone and gave us up,
All the world a daunting and a draining place,
Then in pity and in habit take our cup,
Which we fill with drink, with fire to burn, erase.

And, in bouts of fervour, we are born again,
Toxin turned to mirth; it churns, it swirls, it swells!
Air, once tense, turns light from dark and joy from bane,
And that hope once felled, it rises, stirs; it wells!

Though this drink may be a curse, it is a cure;
It, the motivator for man's love, man's word.
And it's true that all of us were never pure,
So let's drink to be the men we never were!

Starry Hooched Man

Arm up in the air tonight
Reach;
Feel the moon in your palm
Taste the salt of its sores
Relapse, again, the sugars of life
On the burnt pores
What ancient, intense action
Makes delicate unfurling become
The skeleton of flesh, it that quakes
Like a starry hooched man drinking rum

Empty Cup of Cider

Cider can't know what pain is;
No, as I sip, slowly, softly, I pour another,
Amber water come to remind me time has passed.
But it knows pressure, stress,
Oh how it was squeezed, pressed to change!
It was once an apple, many apples; it used to be a lot,
Just like me. I'm a lot right now. I'm just a bunch of apples.
Tumbling around, dirty, compressed, squeezed, toiled, tossed—
The apples become a nectar, but who am I? Strain.
My to-do list is the empty cup next to a gallon of this stuff.
Empty already? Where did all the drink go?
Then I pour another—yes, another.
I fill myself, complete with sweet, earthen dream,
Hundreds of apples rolling and shaking in the basket.
My head wobbles about, eyes darting, fingers twitching—
Oh what does cider know of what it is? What does it say?
Just sweet longings for peace at last?
And I am left with the resonant wish,
Of a still orchard and my place in it—
The cup is empty again
Damnit

II—Desolation

Criticality

(Inspired by Sengai Gibon's death poem)

Simultaneously drained and brimming,
Bubbling void prepared to burst,
This is criticality:
Katsu!
I see it all,
I see the dying corpse,
I see the frailness and loneliness,
I see that it cannot be helped and I cry.
I cry with fermented tears, rich with soiled joy,
I cry with my eyes, with my mouth, with my arms and legs,
I cry out to anyone and everyone hoping that among them
      lie answers;

I cry for a light that no longer burns.
I cling to a cliff, a cloud dissipating.
I know not from where I come.
I know not where I am going.
I know only void.

Split

There he sits, agaze and aimless
      Pupils staggered, raindrop halos
            Distorted sea of fire on sclera

Windowpane drumbeat ripples
      Rainy world peppers hot seeds
            Against the mind, upon the face

Anguish freezes anything good
      Ignites the hellfire trapped in heart
            Become the cloud, hovering, spilling

He reaches for everything at once
      To inflict fury, to embrace in comfort
            The sky is split by lightning, self-infliction

Loss is the unlearning of yourself
      Drowning in a sea of fire and ice
            Looking out the window for someone
                  That will never come to piece you back together

I do not exist

The world is a distant way from here
This which holds the temper of my soul
Where long it ravages with unheard music

The body is cage of wisdom; it knows otherwise
Than to unleash me unto that vastness
For even without it I am lost and fragile

With reluctance, night becomes day, and I
Am charged with ignoring that throb of
Empty space that lingers in my presence

And as day runs from me, my breaths become
Sighs that sit where the sunlight once did
Burning up as wildfire of the forgotten mind

How that blaze takes what flesh I hold and
Scars it with memories of people I once knew
So that the truth of my loneliness is highlighted

You cannot see this world I live in, for it is
Untraceable, wound far around the bent soul
Before it drops off into a chasm that swallows hope

Broken is not enough to describe what I am;
That is a word for something that was once
Whole and together, distinct yet belonging

Fire reflects from out my eyes when I see my
Reflection about an untouchable spirit
That is I, soul forcing life without heart

And this occurs, the unyielding breath sinks
To where it can mourn its own death without
Threat of further ostracization by that world

This world stays busy with itself to forget
The giddy strength of the cosmos, and I hope
One day to form a galaxy reminiscent of reality
Whereby I can ease my way back into the throng
But for now, I do not exist and zeal orients aimlessly

Familial Craving

Pierogi are a metaphor for family—
Gołąbki are a symbol of friendship—
Kaszanka is an emblem of passion—
Pączki are the root of all happiness

Childhood has two meanings:
What happened and what did not happen.

I know myself by the familial craving
Of warm, hearty dishes and sweet, filling desserts.
I know myself by the occasional switch
From English to *that foreign, exciting tongue.*
I know myself by the one excursion
To the country with which I am supposedly kin.
I know myself by the habitudes of my parents,
Passed down from their parents, minute colloquialisms
That remain in my memory, an ancient thing of my ancestors.

At Church, I should feel home, but
Everyone is more fluent than I in what home is.
Here, Poland is a congregation of the faithful; I, too, have faith.

All too familiar, all too distant;
After mass, they talk with blood in their teeth
Red and white
They expect me to understand, but my lost face
Prompts them to ask me if I speak *that foreign, exciting tongue.*

One day

Perhaps if I fill myself up with enough
pierogi, gołąbki, kaszanka, pączki
I can drown away any doubts,
But it won't be enough for me.

I dream about the world where I grew up bilingual,
With relatives overseas that I can be excited to see;
Even then, I am all too distant,
Even now, it is all too familiar.

The world sees my surname and knows immediately who I am,
My family keeps kielbasa in the fridge at all times,
And I see in the mirror those slavic features.

Then why am I stuck on what did not happen?

III—Diplomacy

the night that never ends

Blood.

> A stranger in a banana suit,
> Shirtless students and cans of beer,
> Slutty vampires and nurses,
> Battered in make-up and lipstick,
> Red smeared thoroughly
> Enough.

Children running frantically,
Plastered in scars and scared,

> It's that time of year again, brimming
> With candy and fun for all ages,
> Going from door to door,

For this is indeed a new age,
Where the sun may never rise,
As the night engulfs us all.
They yearn for something sweet,
A moment to relish some peace,

> While amongst families and friends,

Strewn about

> The bodies decorating the lawns,
> Such Halloween cheer, the lights

Glaring and blaring, sirens

        Shrieking with excitement, as

Everyone runs frenzied.
For this is no holiday,
But now it is everyday,
For the children and innocents
Of Palestine and Israel.

              I was sitting at my desk the other night,
              Working on an assignment for astronomy,
              When a splitting headache filled my face
              With unmanageable pain

This was unimaginable.

              I ended up in the hospital

These children never made it to the hospital;

              And then my symptoms went away.
              They told me that I had sinusitis, but
              I think it might have been all in my head.

       I am dressing up for Halloween tonight,
       Going with some friends of mine;
       I have three assignments due and two late.

The world has erupted in ache
Two sides, war and war, terror—

    Panic as emergency services asked me
    If I wanted an ambulance;
    I just want to get better

        For some reason it was 70 degrees
        Fahrenheit these past few days; I wonder if
        We will have a white Christmas this year.
        I can't help but think about
        The wildfires this past summer,

    And I wanted to throw up,

  I was dancing in a costume,

On a night that never ends

        I heard the blue macaws are back, though.
        That's pretty cool. They're beautiful birds.

    I put on "Subwoofer Lullaby" and
    I lay in my bed. I almost feel like I

Never grew up.

Hymn of the People

Glory is a word that carries honour, beauty, pride
    Gory is the state of these old testaments—they died
Loss is all we've gained in these tumultuous years of past
    Oh this ain't gonna stand no more
Our great God is watching us with sorrow in His eyes
    Ready to address the souls that follow the demise
Roaring waves of people as the politicians shake
    You must join us in the fight
Yesterday is gone and now the patriots will rise!

How come all the people are divided and in angst
All the people blind to what another has to say
Love is just a word as hatred conquers heart and tongue
Let the people love once more
Everyone has long forgotten how to be civilised
Losing values has amounted to our nation's cries
Underneath the turmoil our great testaments arise
Justice soon will join our side
And we must act soon, act now
Hell is coming, let us rise!

This Is What You Want to Hear

I know what you want to hear:
The squealing tires of a hundred anxious cars
Racing to their spots by the corporate office
The people yelling profanities about the game
That the celebrities were betting on; watch that money
In the eyes of the gray and smog-eyed citizens
Nothing is enough except what they can do,
And sometimes, that much isn't even enough
The twisted metal spires filled with heavy business
Pierce the wasting atmosphere with authority
And below them scramble a million briefcases
And needles, and hookers, and you as well
This is the truth that you live, it is life
Green means go, means money, means pot
And you mean to whimper in your bubble
Of dirt and broken glass and cigarette butts
But you wait until it pops, because you will find
That the now, the fast-paced, new and rule-breaking
Is what got you there in the first place
Where you can hear but a siren in the distance
And a gunshot five past nine on Sundays

Untouched

Steamboat on the water;
Choking the clear sky, it gives permission
To the ocean to continue its ebb and flow,
The waves cut by the hull, demolition of dance
The breeze spliced as the hunk of future
Grapples its way into the ancient—
And he stands at the helm in a sunbeam: man
His eyes are empty cavities dreaming to burst
Though he is not aware of his fate
This is a culmination since the beginning
The birth of conquest, end of innocence
How shall Earth know itself without scars?
The boat tearing into the skin of the sea
Pluming grey from blue, from green and yellow
Each cloud of smoggy whale carries the plankton
Into tomorrow, that which recalls treasure
As the untouched, now no longer unthought
The ripple effect is the horizon
Everywhere the sky touches—
Anthropocene

IV—Destruction

Past the Beachgrass

The ocean unveils the gritty, endless—
Foot is mussel digging into azure
Moon grasps the flow where I stand
Continuous, ephemeral erasure

It must soon release, to swallow me
I cannot run, for my feet are mussels
My hands are crabs and my eyes are fish
One piece of the salty hustle and bustle

Commotion is a slow and winding breath
Peering through the fated tide as it returns
The cool, blue blood of the hearty ocean
Knows my pain, knows where it burns

I do not wait, there is no expectation
I realise what this world is at its core
I belong some ways past the beachgrass
A speck on the horizon, from the shore

Belong

Cold;
It feels so,
Warm;
My heart is,
Roaring;
The waves are,
There it is
That is where I lie
Deep, deep beyond
The sky or seagrass
Freckles of sand speak
Words about the seagulls
Chit-chat of this or that
Crashing again, for what?
It wants me closer
So my feet drift towards
That icy domain
Peering slowly across
The Earth
—incredibly
Small. I am
There
I keep my pace
And wade through to
Where the sun hides
And the breeze says
Welcome home
As the blue abyss
Engulfs me
And then I am
Cold.

To Answer the Call

Embittered mind enveloped by the flesh—
Therein I hear the call to free that soul.
Emblazoned brain stays oozing in the mesh,
Enraptured by the wound, still warm, still fresh;
Decay ensues by hand, I break that whole.

What comes of wasted body at its end—
Not vigour of the wisp withheld within.
No, this is now disaster none can mend,
How life does call to death, to all they bend;
And still to answer is, as such, a sin!

That Glor'ous Sea

I. Daybreak

What sound so penetrates the dawnlit froth of dew?
How soundly that old robin swarm does sing!
But as the whistling goes, it finds my head askew
And pleasant throb aches into a ringing
I wake to watch this daytime once again renew
And what to this decorum did I bring?
This body that with age has grown a darklit hue
Your highness, it is I, the shadow king

I lift my hurting head from off my breaking bed
That zest of life comes wafting in my face
I smell those roses, as though they're not dead
Each rotting in my garden, a disgrace
I stretch my leaden limbs, restitch that broken thread
And feel the whole grandiose weight of space
The cosmos rests upon my fragile, human head
How can I wake each day and keep good pace?

I peer outside the window, where I see the sun
How hot, how heavily it stares at me!
Those eyes, with godly power they do seem to stun
Having warmed each corner of my body
If only their great heat did not weigh as a ton
As though it is Helios I carry
I look away, and though the daylight brings great fun
It's poison resting in that glor'ous sea

I grab my robe, and tie it 'round my thinning waist
Taking steps out towards my white, beaten door
I reach out gently, then pull at the knob in haste
Scuffling down the hall as though in some war
I've come, and broken as this melancholy waste
Each breath I take a whisper of my gore
That pours from out my soul like it has need to chase
That innocence of life that's left me, sore

As I approach my kitchen, hunger slows my stride
But what I hunger for is out of reach
Contemplation at the breakfast table denied
My body food; my body, or my leech
Who saps me of my self, all that I am, my pride
O vessel, lodged upon this hellish beach
That glor'ous sea awaits for ruination; hide
Within its depths, you see those sins outreach!

With empty stomach, glazed and gaping eyes, I go
And grab my shoes, perhaps a walk will do
That smell of roses real again, how will I know
My demons when the world starts to accrue
The depths do fade away, the land begins to grow
My shoes touch ground, I know that this is true
With hat on head, and gloves on hands, I feel a glow
Of light, and open door, then step on through

II. Reassurance

I never wander far, forget that homely glow
I'm lost enough within this spinning world
At least the glow is there so that I always know
When I return, anxiety is furled
I keep that image in my head, so as I go
As I run, leap, and sprint, as I am whirled
About this land where birds do fly and wind does blow
I'm never truly lost, just somewhat twirled

How spin does seem to fade that harsh and bitter day
And make the world seem like it is afloat
Like planets in the cosmos, as they spin and sway
Untethered, gone and drifting from that moat
That holds the evils of this life, the black and grey
Darkened petrichor gathers as this boat
That sails among the living, in that sunlit bay
And when I wake, it makes way to my throat

But since my wake, that glow has cleansed my broken voice
I sing my song of spinning on this ship
I sail out in that murk, I sail as is my choice
When tired eyes return from tiring trip
Opposing darkness finds itself without its poise
And yet, I am as well, in woozy skip
But I soar on my cosmos where I shall rejoice
Because that black and grey has ceased to grip

That wandering, spinning and singing lifts me high
How like the birds I do so wish to be!
Where sun is more than weight; a beacon in the sky
That scars charred paths into that glor'ous sea
These paths I take, like Moses vested to make wry
Each water droplet rose like doubt did flee
I am my own white dove of peace, from land I fly
To bear unto our good, great God my plea

But as I fly, that spinning makes what's up go down
And dove on path to heaven falls to hell
What was once glowing memory becomes a crown
Of shadow, black and grey begins to well
Sparkling water in that bright sunlit bay turns brown
With every step, the sludge shall churn and swell
I cannot soar in peace, nor swim in murk, I drown
With penetration by that whistling knell

III. Crisis

Each step forward is a step away from comfort
No matter what the route I take or tread
Uneasiness arises; as I move, I hurt
The ache of life descends upon my head
Pushed from above, sucked down below muddy desert
That ghastly, barren void fills me with dread
What miracle can grant to me some great effort
To rise and push along, and march ahead?

None, I say! Not any can, on this glor'ous earth!
I live and ooze each day a nauseous mire
From dawn to dusk, from wake to rest, from coal to hearth
I live a hammered life derived of tire
And moulded on this planet I encounter mirth
But only in those souls with fuel of fire
I am a king of darkness, ocean depths my worth
A slave to sludge and bilge and all things dire

It's everything I've ever truly known; I crave
That glor'ous sea encroaching on my mind
Now body imitates, it moves like one great wave
Arising, pushing up against the rind
Like Eve, and all edenic fruits, I will be brave
All that is good was never good but blind
There is no Garden, rather just one rotten grave
Where bound, my vigour rests with Satan, twined

That calm, that floating emptiness has disappeared
Outwards pushes oceans of my shadow
And down that rainfall pours from out the eyes it's seared
Finally retreating from the shallow
Tears from a time where crying was a sinful fear
Come rushing as if they have need to bellow
That now I'll go about and live a life sincere
Without that Sun glaring on my meadow

While seas do pour, the body makes way to the shore
That glor'ous sea feels anchored by my skin
And I, as well, feel much too anchored to this yore
It's time to be set free, it's time to swim
With rusted iron blade from off my kitchen floor
I hold it close to heart, and on a whim
It pierces flesh, what flesh had naught but all my gore
And sunlight fades, goes dark, and all is dim

Collapsing on the sediment, this sacrifice
To glor'ous sea erects my cold, grave bed
The salt and blood of body is my unpaid price
Living upon this world from which I head
The ocean steals my warmth and turns my head to ice
The spinning slows, and ruptured bides my spirit's thread
My carcass lies in glor'ous sea with this advice;
Life makes of all things easiest to be dead.

V—Development

Break Anew

How many times the rain must pour—
How many, cry I, how much more!
Before we learn to use it well
To wash our bodies, wash our core.

The body lives to weather stress
And stress is weather meant to bless;
How rain comes after heat or drought
To cool the warm and soothe the mess.

There is but naught else one can do
When storm makes way, begins to brew
Than steadfast hold until it breaks
And in the meantime, break anew.

Piano

What comes to mind when pressed
The droplets meeting dirt and grass
The hand lays down its will and
All shocks the sky with thunder
Those fingers, bolts ridden heaven
Melody of wretched earthly anger
Reanimate my spine with profound
Vigour, and the rain yells an echo
Back and down through my flesh
The song is not a song of music
Piano knows the souring of life
And I lay waste to my sorrows

Backlash

And then we halt; the storm
Has come to pass

On the Noon of My 20th Birthday

I sit and watch the trail meander
One part stretching high into the trees
The other down below the rocky shelves
Following the nudge of summer breeze

And here I sit upon a ledge adjacent
For I know not which way I am to go
I supposed if I could watch the gorge
The stream would give me wisdom, let me know

But the water crashes with no eyes
It sees not that I sit here by its side
It does not know to help, or else to harm
And neither does it know to run or hide

It is that it does move itself ahead
But how is it that it knows where to flow?
By and by, it doesn't and will never
Yet I watch it swell, I watch it grow

I sit and watch the trail meander
In time, a yellow jacket flies to me
Startled, I then jump and look about
And think that it just might be time to leave

Bewildered

Bewildered, the Man;

Tasked with the world,
He seizes the universe
And then wonders why
Life is tiring and onerous

But he will come around
When the time is just right
With his arms opened wide
For the world to come nestle

O Man, be wild! O Man, be here!
You are where you belong—
With trust, without fear.

About the Author

C. Walker is a poet born in Switzerland, raised in Connecticut, USA, and pursuing a degree at Cornell University. He is the founder and Editor-in-Chief of *Lucky Lizard Journal,* an egalitarian poetry journal dedicated to poetry of all kinds. He is published in various journals and magazines and has a short story published. He is inspired by writers like W. B. Yeats, Dylan Thomas, Edgar Allan Poe, Rumi, Li Bai, and Robert Frost. When he is not doing poetry, he is usually knee-deep in cosmology research.

Find C. Walker's personal website at:
www.cwalkerpoetry.com

www.ingramcontent.com/pod-product-compliance
Lightning Source LLC
Chambersburg PA
CBHW030916170426
43193CB00009BA/879